THE TWO TIMES TABLE

One times two is two
Two twos are four
Three twos are six
Four twos are eight
Five twos are ten
Six twos are twelve
Seven twos are fourteen
Eight twos are sixteen
Nine twos are eighteen
Ten twos are twenty

1 x 2 =	2
[illegible] x 2 =	4
[illegible] =	6
[illegible]	8
[illegible] =	10
6 x 2 =	12
7 x 2 =	14
8 x 2 =	16
9 x 2 =	18
10 x 2 =	20

Zero times two is zero 0 x 2 = 0

Read the two times table. Try saying it without reading it.
Keep saying it over and over again.

Fill in the missing numbers:

3 x 2 = 6 7 x 2 = 14 9 x 2 = 18 4 x 2 = 8

6 x 2 = 12 2 x 2 = 4 8 x 2 = 16 0 x 2 = 0

10 x 2 = 20 1 x 2 = 2 5 x 2 = 10

Turn to page 2 for more two times table practice.

TWO TIMES TABLE PRACTICE

Fill in the missing answers:

7 x 2 = 14

5 x 2 = 10

2 x 2 = 4

8 x 2 = 16

3 x 2 = 6

6 x 2 = 12

9 x 2 = 18

4 x 2 = 8

0 x 2 = 0

10 x 2 = 20

Draw lines to join the questions to the answers.

9 x 2	16
5 x 2	6
2 x 2	8
8 x 2	20
7 x 2	14
4 x 2	2
3 x 2	18
6 x 2	0
1 x 2	4
0 x 2	10
10 x 2	12

See how quickly you can write out the 2 times table.

The table has been started for you.

1 x 2 = 2

2 x 2 = 4

3 x = 6

4 x = 8

5 x = 10

6 x = 12

7 x = 14

8 x = 16

9 x = 18

10 x = 20

THE THREE TIMES TABLE

One times three is three
Two threes are six
Three threes are nine
Four threes are twelve
Five threes are fifteen
Six threes are eighteen
Seven threes are twenty-one
Eight threes are twenty-four
Nine threes are twenty-seven
Ten threes are thirty

1	x	3	=	3
2	x	3	=	6
3	x	3	=	9
4	x	3	=	12
5	x	3	=	15
6	x	3	=	18
7	x	3	=	21
8	x	3	=	24
9	x	3	=	27
10	x	3	=	30

Zero times three is zero 0 x 3 = 0

Read the three times table.
Can you say it without reading it?

Fill in the missing numbers:

10 x 3 = 30   4 x 3 = 12   7 x 3 = 21   2 x 3 = 6
6 x 3 = 18   0 x 3 = 0   8 x 3 = 24   5 x 3 = 15
1 x 3 = 3   9 x 3 = 27   3 x 3 = 9

Turn to page 4 for more three times table practice.

THREE TIMES TABLE PRACTICE

Fill in the missing answers:

6 x 3 = 18

2 x 3 = 6

9 x 3 = 20

7 x 3 = 21

0 x 3 = 0

10 x 3 = 30

4 x 3 = 12

8 x 3 = 24

5 x 3 = 15

3 x 3 = 9

Draw lines to join the questions to the answers.

4 x 3	15
8 x 3	3
5 x 3	12
10 x 3	0
1 x 3	24
7 x 3	6
0 x 3	27
6 x 3	30
2 x 3	9
9 x 3	18
3 x 3	21

See how quickly you can write out the 3 times table.

The table has been started for you.

1 x 3 = 3

2x = 6

3x = 9

4x = 12

5x = 17

6x = 18

7x = 21

8x = 24

9x = 27

10x = 30

THE FOUR TIMES TABLE

One times four is four
Two fours are eight
Three fours are twelve
Four fours are sixteen
Five fours are twenty
Six fours are twenty-four
Seven fours are twenty-eight
Eight fours are thirty-two
Nine fours are thirty-six
Ten fours are forty

1 x 4 =	4
2 x 4 =	8
3 x 4 =	12
4 x 4 =	16
5 x 4 =	20
6 x 4 =	24
7 x 4 =	28
8 x 4 =	32
9 x 4 =	36
10 x 4 =	40

Zero times four is zero 0 x 4 = 0

Read the four times table.
Keep saying it over and over again.

Fill in the missing numbers:

6 x 4 = ☐ 10 x 4 = ☐ 3 x 4 = ☐ 5 x 4 = ☐

2 x 4 = ☐ 8 x 4 = ☐ 0 x 4 = ☐ 1 x 4 = ☐

4 x 4 = ☐ 9 x 4 = ☐ 7 x 4 = ☐

Turn to page 6 for more four times table practice.

FOUR TIMES TABLE PRACTICE

Fill in the missing answers:

3 x 4 = ☐

9 x 4 = ☐

2 x 4 = ☐

6 x 4 = ☐

10 x 4 = ☐

5 x 4 = ☐

0 x 4 = ☐

8 x 4 = ☐

4 x 4 = ☐

7 x 4 = ☐

Draw lines to join the questions to the answers.

6 x 4	40
1 x 4	4
9 x 4	12
3 x 4	24
4 x 4	20
10 x 4	32
2 x 4	36
8 x 4	8
5 x 4	16
7 x 4	0
0 x 4	28

1 x 4 = 4

THE FIVE TIMES TABLE

One times five is five
Two fives are ten
Three fives are fifteen
Four fives are twenty
Five fives are twenty-five
Six fives are thirty
Seven fives are thirty-five
Eight fives are forty
Nine fives are forty-five
Ten fives are fifty

1 x 5 = 5
2 x 5 = 10
3 x 5 = 15
4 x 5 = 20
5 x 5 = 25
6 x 5 = 30
7 x 5 = 35
8 x 5 = 40
9 x 5 = 45
10 x 5 = 50

Zero times five is zero 0 x 5 = 0

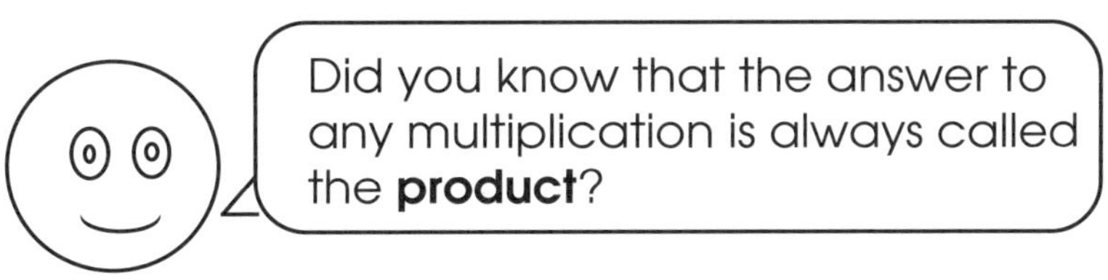

Fill in the missing products of five:

5, 10 , 15 , ☐ , 25 , 30 , ☐ , 40 , 45 , ☐

3 x 5 = ☐ 7 x 5 = ☐ 4 x 5 = ☐ 9 x 5 = ☐

Turn to page 8 for more five times table practice.

FIVE TIMES TABLE PRACTICE

Fill in the missing answers:

5 x 5 = ☐

0 x 5 = ☐

8 x 5 = ☐

3 x 5 = ☐

10 x 5 = ☐

6 x 5 = ☐

2 x 5 = ☐

7 x 5 = ☐

4 x 5 = ☐

9 x 5 = ☐

Draw lines to join the questions to the answers.

9 x 5	25
5 x 5	0
2 x 5	10
8 x 5	30
0 x 5	50
6 x 5	45
3 x 5	20
10 x 5	5
4 x 5	15
7 x 5	40
1 x 5	35

See how quickly you can write out the 5 times table.

The table has been started for you.

1 x 5 = 5

THE SIX TIMES TABLE

One times six is six
Two sixes are twelve
Three sixes are eighteen
Four sixes are twenty-four
Five sixes are thirty
Six sixes are thirty-six
Seven sixes are forty-two
Eight sixes are forty-eight
Nine sixes are fifty-four
Ten sixes are sixty

1 x 6 = 6
2 x 6 = 12
3 x 6 = 18
4 x 6 = 24
5 x 6 = 30
6 x 6 = 36
7 x 6 = 42
8 x 6 = 48
9 x 6 = 54
10 x 6 = 60

Zero times six is zero 0 x 6 = 0

Read the six times table.
Say it again and again.

Fill in the missing numbers:

6 x 6 =	2 x 6 =	10 x 6 =	
8 x 6 =	3 x 6 =	7 x 6 =	4 x 6 =
0 x 6 =	5 x 6 =	1 x 6 =	9 x 6 =

Turn to page 10 for more six times table practice.

SIX TIMES TABLE PRACTICE

Fill in the missing answers:

10 x 6 = ☐

3 x 6 = ☐

7 x 6 = ☐

4 x 6 = ☐

8 x 6 = ☐

2 x 6 = ☐

1 x 6 = ☐

9 x 6 = ☐

5 x 6 = ☐

6 x 6 = ☐

Draw lines to join the questions to the answers.

2 x 6	24
5 x 6	18
9 x 6	12
4 x 6	42
8 x 6	0
0 x 6	6
6 x 6	30
3 x 6	48
1 x 6	60
7 x 6	36
10 x 6	54

THE SEVEN TIMES TABLE

One times seven is seven
Two sevens are fourteen
Three sevens are twenty-one
Four sevens are twenty-eight
Five sevens are thirty-five
Six sevens are forty-two
Seven sevens are forty-nine
Eight sevens are fifty-six
Nine sevens are sixty-three
Ten sevens are seventy

1 x 7 = 7
2 x 7 = 14
3 x 7 = 21
4 x 7 = 28
5 x 7 = 35
6 x 7 = 42
7 x 7 = 49
8 x 7 = 56
9 x 7 = 63
10 x 7 = 70

Zero times seven is zero 0 x 7 = 0

Keep practising the seven times table.

Fill in the missing products of seven:

7 , 14, 21 , ___ , 35 , ___ , 49 , ___ , ___ , 70

3 x 7 = ___ 7 x 7 = ___ 2 x 7 = ___ 4 x 7 = ___

10 x 7 = ___ 0 x 7 = ___ 8 x 7 = ___ 6 x 7 = ___

Turn over the page for more seven times table practice.

SEVEN TIMES TABLE PRACTICE

Fill in the missing answers:

9 x 7 =

2 x 7 =

5 x 7 =

1 x 7 =

8 x 7 =

6 x 7 =

10 x 7 =

3 x 7 =

7 x 7 =

4 x 7 =

Draw lines to join the questions to the answers.

7 x 7	70
9 x 7	28
1 x 7	42
4 x 7	7
6 x 7	56
2 x 7	49
10 x 7	14
5 x 7	21
8 x 7	0
0 x 7	63
3 x 7	35

See how quickly you can write out the 7 times table.

Start with 1 x 7.

THE EIGHT TIMES TABLE

One times eight is eight
Two eights are sixteen
Three eights are twenty-four
Four eights are thirty-two
Five eights are forty
Six eights are forty-eight
Seven eights are fifty-six
Eight eights are sixty-four
Nine eights are seventy-two
Ten eights are eighty

$1 \times 8 = 8$
$2 \times 8 = 16$
$3 \times 8 = 24$
$4 \times 8 = 32$
$5 \times 8 = 40$
$6 \times 8 = 48$
$7 \times 8 = 56$
$8 \times 8 = 64$
$9 \times 8 = 72$
$10 \times 8 = 80$

Zero times eight is zero $0 \times 8 = 0$

Keep reading the eight times table to learn it.

Fill in the missing numbers:

$6 \times 8 = \square$ $9 \times 8 = \square$ $2 \times 8 = \square$ $0 \times 8 = \square$

$3 \times 8 = \square$ $10 \times 8 = \square$ $1 \times 8 = \square$ $4 \times 8 = \square$

$7 \times 8 = \square$ $5 \times 8 = \square$ $8 \times 8 = \square$

Turn to page 14 for more eight times table practice.

EIGHT TIMES TABLE PRACTICE

Fill in the missing answers:

8 x 8 =

5 x 8 =

2 x 8 =

7 x 8 =

4 x 8 =

10 x 8 =

6 x 8 =

3 x 8 =

9 x 8 =

1 x 8 =

Draw lines to join the questions to the answers.

10 x 8	32
2 x 8	0
0 x 8	48
6 x 8	16
9 x 8	24
4 x 8	8
7 x 8	80
3 x 8	40
8 x 8	56
1 x 8	72
5 x 8	64

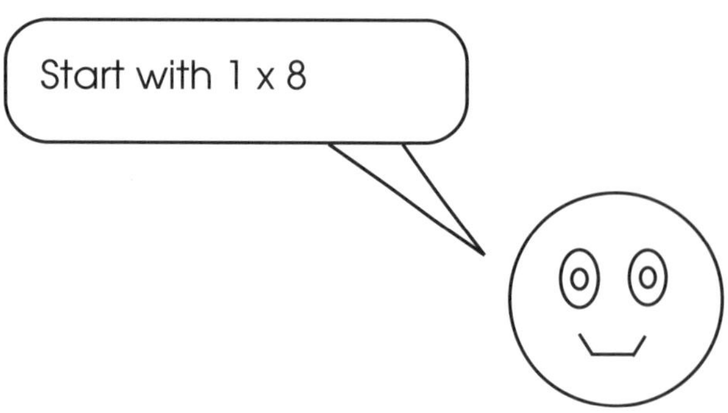

THE NINE TIMES TABLE

One times nine is nine
Two nines are eighteen
Three nines are twenty-seven
Four nines are thirty-six
Five nines are forty-five
Six nines are fifty-four
Seven nines are sixty-three
Eight nines are seventy-two
Nine nines are eighty-one
Ten nines are ninety

1 x 9 = 9
2 x 9 = 18
3 x 9 = 27
4 x 9 = 36
5 x 9 = 45
6 x 9 = 54
7 x 9 = 63
8 x 9 = 72
9 x 9 = 81
10 x 9 = 90

Zero times nine is zero 0 x 9 = 0

Learn the nine times table by reading it over and over again. Now try saying it without reading it.

Fill in the missing numbers:

7 x 9 = ☐ 3 x 9 = ☐ 1 x 9 = ☐ 9 x 9 = ☐

4 x 9 = ☐ 0 x 9 = ☐ 2 x 9 = ☐ 8 x 9 = ☐

10 x 9 = ☐ 5 x 9 = ☐ 6 x 9 = ☐

There's more nine times table practice on page 16

NINE TIMES TABLE PRACTICE

Fill in the missing answers:

0 x 9 =

7 x 9 =

5 x 9 =

2 x 9 =

9 x 9 =

6 x 9 =

10 x 9 =

3 x 9 =

8 x 9 =

4 x 9 =

Draw lines to join the questions to the answers.

6 x 9	27
1 x 9	36
9 x 9	90
3 x 9	81
7 x 9	54
10 x 9	18
4 x 9	9
8 x 9	0
5 x 9	72
0 x 9	45
2 x 9	63

See how quickly you can write out the 9 times table.

You could time yourself with a watch or a clock.

THE TEN TIMES TABLE

One times ten is ten
Two tens are twenty
Three tens are thirty
Four tens are forty
Five tens are fifty
Six tens are sixty
Seven tens are seventy
Eight tens are eighty
Nine tens are ninety

1 x 10 = 10
2 x 10 = 20
3 x 10 = 30
4 x 10 = 40
5 x 10 = 50
6 x 10 = 60
7 x 10 = 70
8 x 10 = 80
9 x 10 = 90

Ten tens are a hundred 10 x 10 = 100

Zero times ten is zero 0 x 10 = 0

The ten times table is the easiest table to learn.
Answer these questions without looking at the table:

3 x 10 = ☐ 6 x 10 = ☐ 4 x 10 = ☐ 0 x 10 = ☐

5 x 10 = ☐ 8 x 10 = ☐ 2 x 10 = ☐ 9 x 10 = ☐

1 x 10 = ☐ 7 x 10 = ☐ 10 x 10 = ☐

Turn to page 18 for more multiplications of ten.

TEN TIMES TABLE PRACTICE

Fill in the missing answers:

3 x 10 = ☐

5 x 10 = ☐

2 x 10 = ☐

7 x 10 = ☐

1 x 10 = ☐

6 x 10 = ☐

4 x 10 = ☐

9 x 10 = ☐

0 x 10 = ☐

8 x 10 = ☐

Draw lines to join the questions to the answers.

10 x 10	50
3 x 10	60
8 x 10	0
1 x 10	40
5 x 10	30
4 x 10	70
0 x 10	100
9 x 10	80
6 x 10	10
2 x 10	90
7 x 10	20

See how quickly you can write out the 10 times table.

Can you write it in less than one minute?

____

____

____

____

____

____

____

____

____

____

0 x 11 =	0
1 x 11 =	11
2 x 11 =	22
3 x 11 =	33
4 x 11 =	44
5 x 11 =	55
6 x 11 =	66
7 x 11 =	77
8 x 11 =	88
9 x 11 =	99
10 x 11 =	110
11 x 11 =	121
12 x 11 =	132

THE ELEVEN TIMES TABLE

One times eleven is eleven
Two elevens are twenty-two
Three elevens are thirty-three
Four elevens are forty-four
Five elevens are fifty-five
Six elevens are sixty-six
Seven elevens are seventy-seven
Eight elevens are eighty-eight
Nine elevens are ninety-nine
Ten elevens are one hundred and ten
Eleven elevens are a hundred and twenty-one
Twelve elevens are a hundred and thirty-two

Fill in the missing numbers:

6 x 11= ☐ 7 x 11 = ☐ 9 x 11 = ☐ 11 x 11 = ☐

5 x 11 = ☐ 12 x 11 = ☐ 10 x 11 = ☐

Turn to page 21 for the twelve times table.

ELEVEN TIMES TABLE PRACTICE

Fill in the missing products of eleven:

11, ____, 33, ____, ____, ____,

77, ____, 99, ____, 121, ____.

Fill in the missing answers:

12 x 11 = ____

6 x 11 = ____

4 x 11 = ____

9 x 11 = ____

2 x 11 = ____

7 x 11 = ____

10 x 11 = ____

8 x 11 = ____

5 x 11 = ____

0 x 11 = ____

11 x 11 = ____

3 x 11 = ____

1 x 11 = ____

THE TWELVE TIMES TABLE

0	x	12	=	0
1	x	12	=	12
2	x	12	=	24
3	x	12	=	36
4	x	12	=	48
5	x	12	=	60
6	x	12	=	72
7	x	12	=	84
8	x	12	=	96
9	x	12	=	108
10	x	12	=	120
11	x	12	=	132
12	x	12	=	144

One times twelve is twelve
Two twelves are twenty-four
Three twelves are thirty-six
Four twelves are forty-eight
Five twelves are sixty
Six twelves are seventy-two
Seven twelves are eighty-four
Eight twelves are ninety-six
Nine twelves are a hundred and eight
Ten twelves are a hundred and twenty
Eleven twelves are a hundred and thirty-two
Twelve twelves are a hundred and forty-four

Fill in the missing numbers:

☐ x 12 = 84 ☐ x 12 = 36 ☐ x 12 = 132

☐ x 12 = 96 ☐ x 12 = 48 ☐ x 12 = 144

☐ x 12 = 0 ☐ x 12 = 60 ☐ x 12 = 120

Turn over for lots more tables practice.

TWELVE TIMES TABLE PRACTICE

Fill in the missing products of twelve:

12 , ___ , 36, ___ , 60 , ___ , 84 ,

96 , ___ , ___ , ___ , 144

Fill in the missing answers:

6 x 12 = ☐

1 x 12 = ☐

9 x 12 = ☐

4 x 12 = ☐

12 x 12 = ☐

7 x 12 = ☐

2 x 12 = ☐

10 x 12 = ☐

0 x 12 = ☐

8 x 12 = ☐

5 x 12 = ☐

11 x 12 = ☐

3 x 12 = ☐

Write out the twelve times table as quickly as you can.

PRACTISE ALL YOUR TABLES

How quickly can you write each table?

2 x table

x =
x =
x =
x =
x =
x =
x =
x =
x =
x =

Time taken: [ ] seconds.

3 x table

x =
x =
x =
x =
x =
x =
x =
x =
x =
x =

Time taken: [ ] seconds.

4 x table

x =
x =
x =
x =
x =
x =
x =
x =
x =
x =

Time taken: [ ] seconds.

5 x table

x =
x =
x =
x =
x =
x =
x =
x =
x =
x =

Time taken: [ ] seconds.

6 x table

x =
x =
x =
x =
x =
x =
x =
x =
x =
x =

Time taken: [ ] seconds.

7 x table

x =
x =
x =
x =
x =
x =
x =
x =
x =
x =

Time taken: [ ] seconds.

8 x table

x =
x =
x =
x =
x =
x =
x =
x =
x =
x =

Time taken:
seconds.

9 x table

x =
x =
x =
x =
x =
x =
x =
x =
x =
x =

Time taken:
seconds.

10 x table

x =
x =
x =
x =
x =
x =
x =
x =
x =
x =

Time taken:
seconds.

11 x table

x =
x =
x =
x =
x =
x =
x =
x =
x =
x =
x =
x =

Time taken:
seconds.

12 x table

x =
x =
x =
x =
x =
x =
x =
x =
x =
x =
x =
x =

Time taken:
seconds.